DETECTIVE TOM MATO PASTE

And the Case of the Bad Cheese

Written by Gabby Walker
Illustrated by Ashton McDonald
& Gabby Walker

Copyright ©Gabby Walker 2023 All Rights Reserved

ISBN: 978-1-943201-93-8

Library of Congress Control Number: 2022941794

All rights reserved. No part of this book may be reproduced or transmitted in any form or by any means, electronic or mechanical, including photocopying, recording, or by any information storage and retrieval system, without permission in writing from the publisher.

First Published by AM Ink Publishing LLC, Southwick, MA 2023

www.AMInkPublishing.com

Sometimes at night, do you lie down and **think**,
what goes on in that fridge that's right by the **sink**?
Does all your food sit still until your family wakes **up**,
Or does it all come to life when the fridge door is **shut**?

Now you might not believe me, but I've seen it before.

They do come alive when we close our fridge door;

The fruits, the veggies, the meats, and the dairy.

And most of the time they are all quite merry.

See, when good food is good there's fun to be **had**,

But good times turn stale when good food goes **bad**.

This sort of thing happens every now and **again**.

A good food turns bad and bad mouths his **friends**.

When a good food goes bad he turns a strange color,

His smell is quite smelly and your nose you must cover.

When a good food goes bad his stink is a stank,

He never says "please"; he never says "thanks".

It happened last night to a nice wheel of cheese.

He began to smell bad and his yellow turned green.

His attitude changed, and he sure became rotten.

He made fun of some foods, and started causing a problem.

He then ran and hid and disguised his face.

He grew out his beard and started wearing a cape.

The other foods called a tin can who would take on the case.

His name was Detective Tom Mato, Tom Mato Paste.

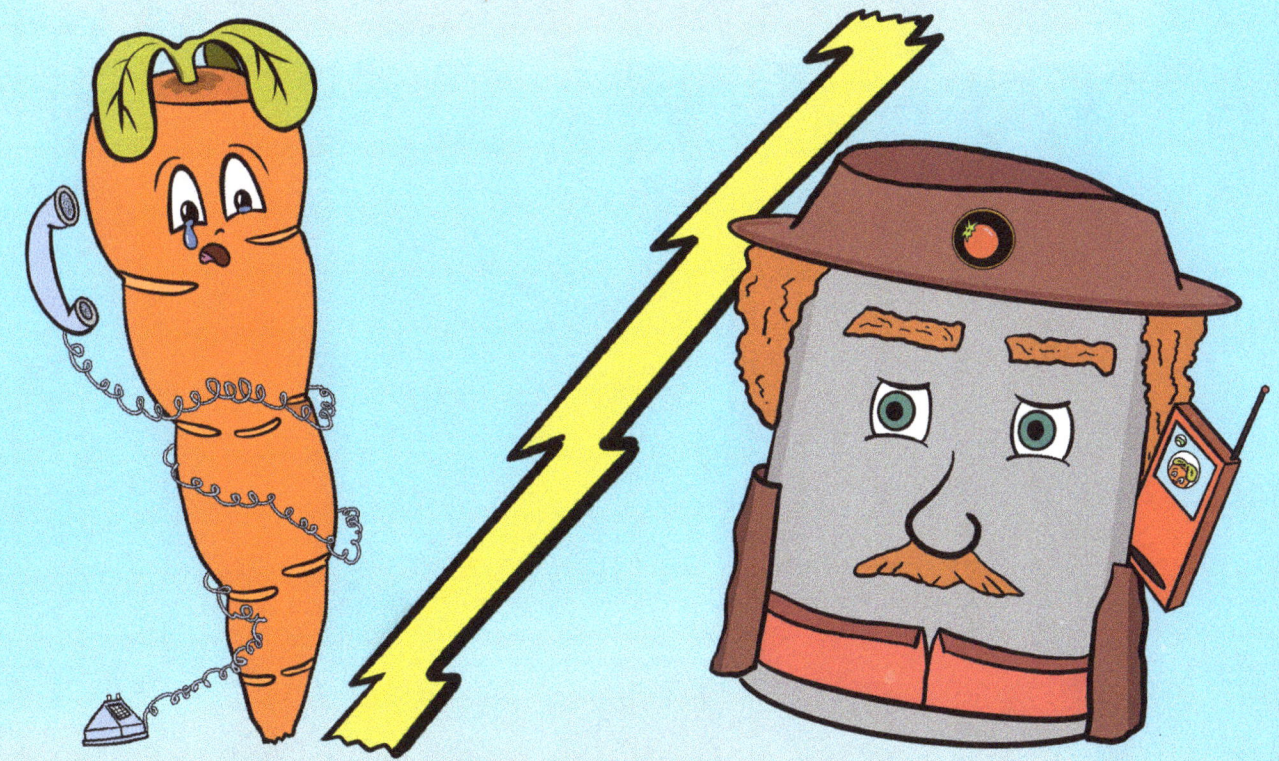

Tom said "I'll take on this case, I know just what I'll do.

I'll convince this cheese, He doesn't belong with us food."

"But first thing is first, this cheese must be found.

I'll start at the top and work my way down.

On the top shelf I'll meet with a lass named Miss Butter,

A smooth young gal who speaks like no other."

Every word Miss Butter muttered,

Was uttered with a stutter,

But her voice was so cute,

You couldn't help but love her.

Well Tom talked to **her,**

Her mother, and her **brothers,**

They said, "The cheese was just **there,**

With the honey and the **mustard."**

Next Tom met with a nice bottle of honey,

Who wore overalls and talked kind of funny.

The honey said, "Listen here, bud. I don't belong in this place,

I left the pantry tonight to spend time with the grapes,

I ain't been with that mustard, you must have heard wrong.

But I smelled something stinking, something so strong.

It came from down under this shelf I say please,

Go down there Tom and make that cheese leave."

The next shelf was packed with a very close crew.
They all stuck together. It was a family of fruits.
Tom had never seen any fruits that had more glamour,
Than the seventeen grapes, all named Savannah.

The Savannahs would argue and were always up late,

Tom knew they were wild even for grapes,

But on that night the Savannahs agreed,

"Like yeah, we've seen that really mean cheese."

"Those Savannahs were dancing; they were cutting a rug.

These Savannahs were chatting with some raisins they love.

That Savannah right there, was with a hand of bananas,

And this Savannah was jamming with two pears in bandanas."

"The cheese walked in and said our party's no fun,

He said we just whine, and he said he was done,

He said he was leaving, and about to go find,

Some veggies and give them a piece of his mind."

Next Tom met with a lonely stalk of broccoli,

Who wore a black belt and talked only of karate.

He said, "Yeah I saw a cheese, I think he was rotting,

I forgot he even saw me. I was practicing karate,

But he said my stance was sloppy,

And my chops were way too choppy."

Then that karate-loving broccoli,

Said "You can catch him probably!

He said he was on his way to where it's always frosty,

And I really do believe, the freezer is what he means."

Tom went to the freezer,

Do you know what he saw?

Tom saw Mr. Ice-Cream,

And he was standing in frost.

"MY NAME IS ICE-CREAM,

AND I SCREAM WHAT I SAY!

I'VE SEEN THAT GREEN CHEESE,

I'VE SEEN HIM TODAY!"

"I'LL TELL YOU MISTER TOM,

HE HAD MY BRAIN IN A KNOT.

HE SAID WE ARE BROTHERS,

BUT I KNOW THAT WE'RE NOT."

"I KNOW MY TWO BROTHERS,

MILK AND WHIPPED CREAM,

AND MY SIS IS MISS BUTTER,

BUT NONE OF THEM ARE LIGHT GREEN!"

"HE'S RIGHT OVER THERE,

HE'S RIGHT ON THIS SHELF!

GO SEE HIM TOM,

THAT CHEESE NEEDS SOME HELP!"

"Stop right there! And listen you cheese,

You don't belong here, and not just cause you'll freeze,

But also because, you're no longer a food.

Go wait in the trash; I know a place just for you."

"The trash will be taken to a place called the dump,

But don't be afraid my old dairy chum.

See you're not one of us, and it's making you sour,

But things will be better in a matter of hours.

So say your goodbyes but this isn't the end.

You'll go to a new place and meet some new friends.

You'll have a good time and you really deserve it.

So go to the trash and stop acting so nervous."

The Cheese left quick, he rolled away in a **flash.**

He jumped out of the fridge and fell straight in the **trash.**

For the first time that night the cheese had a **smile,**

He would see his new family in a short little **while.**

The sun came up, and the foods were all **glad,**

That Tom found a new home for the cheese that turned **bad.**

So glad, in fact, they threw him a giant food **party,**

Since Tom solved the case and the cheese had said **"sorry".**

And do you know who was there, a new wheel of **cheese.**

Who used her manners, and was as nice as can **be.**

So there you have it friends, and now you do know,
What happens at night when the fridge door is closed.
When good food is good there's fun to be had,
But good times turn stale when good food goes bad.
And if good food turns bad, please don't be afraid,
Detective Tom Mato will always take on the case.

To my fiancé and co-illustrator, Ashton McDonald, thank you for laughing at the idea of this story on our first date. I couldn't have made it a reality without you. I promise I'll never ask you to draw another food again.

To my parents and siblings, thank you for always being supportive of my creative endeavors.

To my nieces, Frankie and Rosie, and my nephew, Holden, thank you for being my focus group. I will not forget the feeling of being on pins and needles as you carefully reviewed each page.

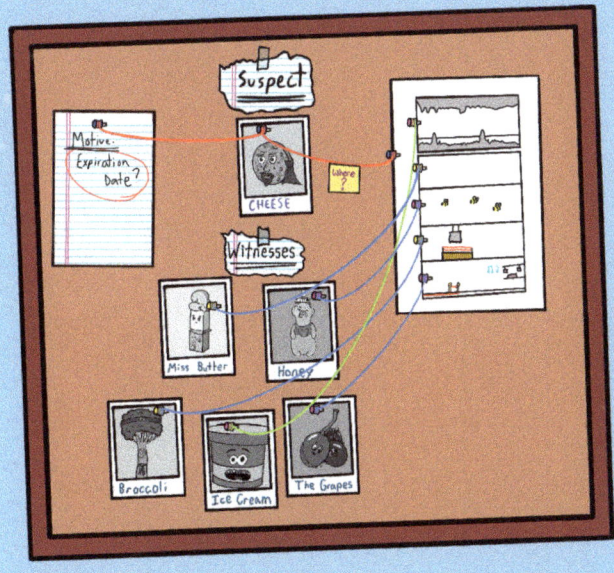

CPSIA information can be obtained
at www.ICGtesting.com
Printed in the USA
BVHW011552300323
661463BV00002B/2